DOCTOR

Rebecca Hunter

**Photography by
Chris Fairclough**

CHERRYTREE BOOKS

A Cherrytree book

Published by
Evans Brothers Ltd
2A Portman Mansions
Chiltern Street
London W1U 6NR

Reprinted in 2007, 2009

British Library Cataloguing in Publication Data
Hunter, Rebecca
  Doctor. - (People who help us)
  1. Physicians - Juvenile literature
  I. Title
  610. 6'95

ISBN 9781842342978

Planned and produced by Discovery Books Ltd
Editor: Rebecca Hunter
Designer: Ian Winton

Acknowledgements
Commissioned photography by Chris Fairclough.

The author, packager and publisher would like to thank Dr Fiona Clare, the staff and patients of the Caledonian Road Medical Centre and Graeme, Hamish, Catriona and Isobel Houston for their participation in this book.

Words appearing in bold like this, are explained in the glossary.

Contents

I am a doctor

My name is Fiona.
I am a doctor.

This is where I work. It is called the Caledonian Road Medical Centre and is in the city of Perth in Scotland.

I am one of seven doctors who work in this practice.

8.00 I arrive at work.

5

The medical centre

I say hello to Brenda. She is the receptionist and welcomes the patients to the medical centre. She gives me some notes and a few messages.

Next I go to my room and switch on my computer. I look at my post.

The waiting room is full of patients who are waiting for morning surgery to begin.

There is a special area with toys and games where children can play.

The first patient

I go to the waiting room and call my first patient.

Anna has earache. I need to look inside her ear but Anna is a bit nervous. To make her feel better we pretend her toy rabbit has a sore ear!

Now I look inside Anna's ear. I use my auroscope. I can see that she has an infection.

I give her mother a prescription. She can take this to the chemist and get some medicine to make Anna's ear better.

Back ache

My next patient is Linda.

She explains that she has a pain in her back.

I move her leg and she tells me when it hurts. I can then work out what is causing the pain.

This is a model of the human backbone.
I show Linda where her problem is.

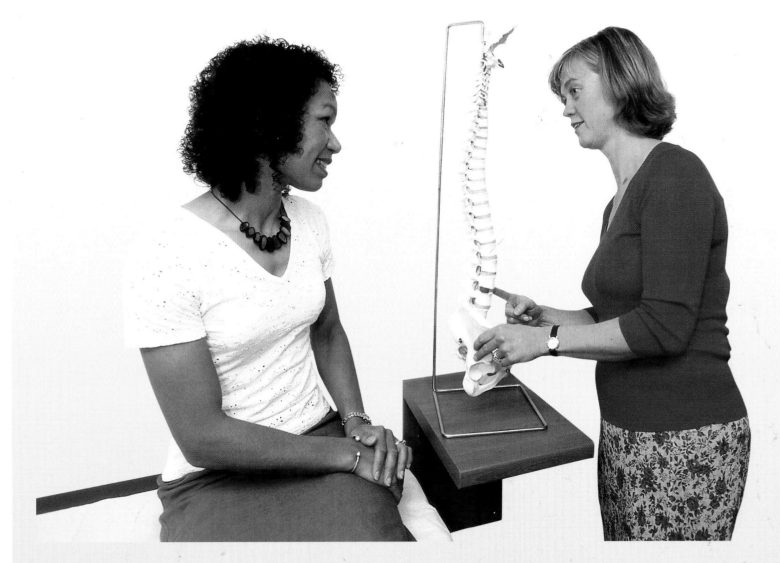

She has pulled some muscles in her back.
She will need to go to see the
physiotherapist who also works here.

Up to the office

11.00 I go upstairs to the office area. On the way I meet Sandra, one of the **district nurses**. She asks me about a patient.

In the office I make a phone call. I need to talk to one of the doctors at the hospital.

This is where the patients' records are stored. There are over 10,000 sets of case notes here. All these notes will soon be computerized. It will make my job much easier!

The office manager asks me about a patient who has called to get the results of a test.

Lunchtime

Before lunch I have a meeting with some of the other doctors. This is often the only time we can discuss things. We are thinking of taking on a student doctor.

Now it is lunchtime! Because I live nearby I can walk home for lunch.

I make myself a quick snack and then I take my dogs for a walk. It is nice to get some fresh air in the middle of the day.

House calls

This afternoon I am going out to make some house calls. I take my doctor's bag with me. It contains a lot of useful things.

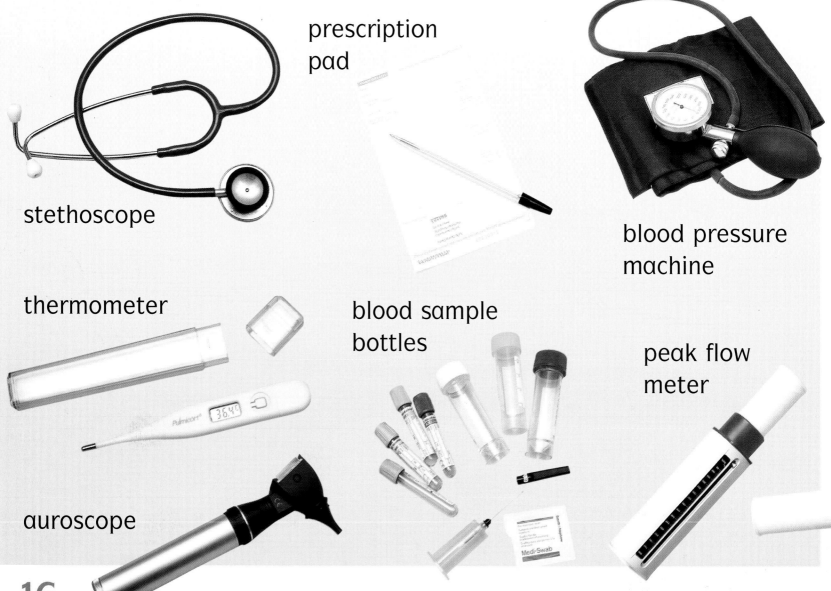

stethoscope

prescription pad

blood pressure machine

thermometer

blood sample bottles

peak flow meter

auroscope

The first patient
I am going to
see lives in this
block of flats.

She has been very poorly.
I ask her how she feels
today and give her a
prescription for some
more medicine.

The baby clinic

Seth, the **health visitor**, does an afternoon baby clinic. Today Elspeth has brought in her baby Jonny. He needs a **vaccination** but his mother is a bit worried because he has a cough.

Seth asks me to check the baby's chest. I listen with my **stethoscope**. I tell them he is well enough to have the vaccination.

Seth weighs the baby on the scales. Jonny thinks it is fun.

Finally Seth gives Jonny his injection.

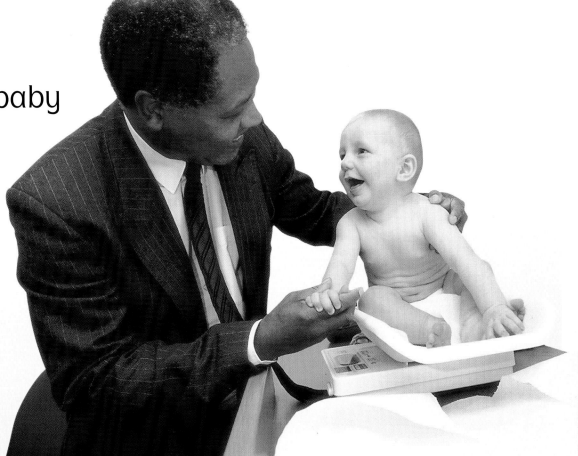

Jonny does not like it very much, but it will stop him getting diseases such as measles and mumps as he grows up.

Asthma

My last patient today is Hamish. He has asthma. His dad has brought him in because he has been wheezing. Hamish tells me that his chest hurts and it is difficult for him to breathe properly.

I ask him to blow into a peak flow meter. This tells me how bad his asthma is.

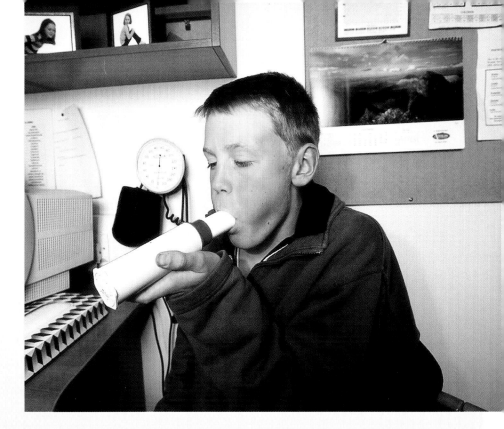

I send Hamish to see the practice nurse. She checks he is using his inhaler properly.

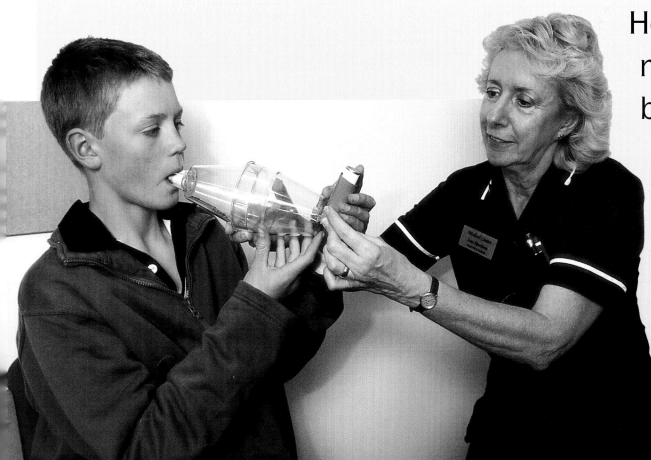

Hamish will need to come back to our asthma clinic so we can check on his progress.

At home

Today has been a busy day but it is not over yet. After I finish work I collect my daughters from school. When we get home I make them tea and then help them with their homework.

Both my children want to be doctors. They know that it is a hard but rewarding job and they can see how much I enjoy it.

THE LEARNING CENTRE
TOWER HAMLETS COLLEGE
ARBOUR SQUARE
LONDON E1 0PS

Glossary

asthma a disease of the chest that causes wheezing and makes it hard to breathe

auroscope an instrument for looking inside the ear

case notes written information about a patient's medical history

district nurse a nurse who looks after people in their homes

health visitor a person who works at keeping people healthy

house calls visits made to a patient at home by a doctor

patients people who need to receive treatment from a doctor

physiotherapist a person who treats injuries by massaging the body

practice the business of a doctor or lawyer

prescription a written note from the doctor that tells the chemist what medicine to give the person

receptionist the person who welcomes visitors, answers the telephone and arranges appointments

stethoscope an instrument for listening to the heart and breathing

surgery the time when doctors see patients who have made appointments

vaccination an injection that protects against disease

wheezing breathing with difficulty, making a whistling sound

Index